Dear Strong Black Woman

Letters of nourishment and reflection
from one strong black woman to another

Jennifer Sterling

ONE IDEA PRESS  PITTSBURGH

Printed in the United States
ONE IDEA PRESS
Pittsburgh, PA
OneIdeaPress.com

ISBN: 978-1-944134-21-1

Printed in the United States of America

For information, special sales, premium, custom, and corporate purchases, please contact One Idea Press at hello@oneideapress.com.

DEAR STRONG BLACK WOMAN

Jennifer Sterling

praise *from* Strong Black Women

"I have never read ANYTHING that has made me feel this SEEN. It's the sweetest love letter to those who are a rock for everyone else, but who are often taken for granted. *Dear Strong Black Woman* dares to disrupt what we've been taught about self-love and self-care. This book is a literary balm, soothing mind, body and spirit. I can't wait to gift it to all of the Strong Black Women that I know."
-Peachie Wimbush-Polk

"A real life depiction of every black woman's struggle and strength. Each letter captures the essence of a black woman's heart."
-Ta'lor L. Pinkston, *The Heart Advocate*

a note
about the artwork in this book:

The artwork in this book was created through intentional movements by strong black women at a Yoga Paint Party™ by YOGAMOTIF, which invites participants to use their bodies as paintbrushes to create a mess-free painting on their yoga mats.

Special thanks to:
Zoe Vivienne Young, 3
Alecia Dawn Young,
Founder of YOGAMOTIF, 34
Heather Louise Manning, 37
Roxanne Easley, 42
Tereneh Idia, 50

For more information on Yoga Paint Party™:
www.yogamotif.com

If you want something done, you have to do it yourself.

If I had a philosophy on life, that was it. It wasn't a philosophy I chose, however. It was one that had been passed down from one woman in my family to another. One that was repeated with such conviction, over and over again, that it became our truth.

Well, that and it also served as our incredibly high expectation of how things should be done.

This philosophy and our unwavering belief in it is what made us strong black women—women who could do anything and everything ourselves, women who never asked for help.

Of course, it would have been nice to have help at times, but once people perceive you as strong, they stop offering. They assume that you can do everything on your own because that's the way it's always been.

Most of my life, that was the case. No matter what challenges life threw at me, I figured them out, from homelessness to racist college professors and employers, to motherhood, and everything in between. While I'm proud of myself for making a dollar out of fifteen cents, being independent, and not giving up when times got tough, I do wish I could have asked for help more often—about twenty-five years earlier than I did.

Asking for help may have saved me from the hunger pangs of having no food to eat, from throbbing migraines that lasted for days, and from countless depressive episodes that I wasn't sure would end.

That "maybe" is why I'm writing these letters to you, strong black woman.

I want you to know that while our strength is admirable and unparalleled, it's okay to also be soft, and asking for help does not make you any less strong or independent.

We live in a world where we, as black women, are expected to always be strong, take care of everyone before ourselves. If we want to continue to be well, however, we have to shift the paradigm.

We must ask for and allow others to pour into us in the same way we've poured into them. We must make space for nourishment in our lives, physically, mentally, and emotionally.

This doesn't make us less strong. In fact, it does the opposite. It makes us more vital, more well, and even more resilient.

Dear Strong Black Woman, please read these words and know that I see you, and I'm rooting for your wellness.

Dear Strong Black Woman,

Wear your strength like a badge of honor, proudly.

Stand tall, like all the women who came before you.

Own your magic: the ability to turn fifteen cents into a dollar, raise a child on your own, feed your community, climb the highest of heights to remove symbols of racism and oppression...

Save the world, if you have to.

You can do it all without batting an eyelash or letting anyone see you cry, because emotions aren't allowed when you're strong—people are depending on you to hold them up, inspire them, save them.

There's no time for tears or weakness.

I know you can do it, Strong Black Woman. This is the way it's always been done.

We have a long lineage that makes the need to be strong feel like your responsibility—enslaved females were expected to care for other slaves while being whipped and carrying their enslaver's babies. Modern day doctors expect you to feel less pain than a white woman.

And while most days you can press on, remain functional.
There are other days when it feels like you're drowning in a sea of unexpressed emotion.

Hopeless.

But this time,
instead of bearing the burden all by yourself,
and burying your emotions until you start to feel like a shell of yourself...

Find a safe space, take off your cape... release the weight... breathe.
And if you can muster the energy, *treat yourself well.*

Dear Strong Black Woman,

Where did you get your strength?

Did you inherit it from your mother, your grandmother, your aunt?

Did they show you all the ways they could work tirelessly
        ...bending,
                    ...and bending,
                                ...and bending over backwards,
for everyone but themselves?

Did you watch them negotiate this white supremacist, capitalist, patriarchal society—study all their tricks, adopt their mannerisms, and know that you would need to use them one day to survive?

Your strength, Strong Black Woman.

Tell me, where did it come from?

Dear Strong Black Woman,

Society would have us believe that we are less than human.

Ugly.

Unintelligent.

Unworthy.

Unclean.

But you know as well as I that our melanin makes us who we are.
Through trials and tribulations in history, it has made us a strong and beautifully resilient people.

There is nothing wrong with you, Strong Black Woman.
It is the world we live in that is broken.

Dear Strong Black Woman,

Did you know that trauma can be passed down through your DNA?

The beatings, lynchings, separation from loved ones didn't end with the
Emancipation Proclamation and Martin Luther King, Jr., and instead,
live in our bodies.

These experiences have been passed down from one generation of black people to
the next in body, mind, and action—

> We are more prone to heart disease,
> more likely to be depressed than white women,
> some of us still whip our children in the name of discipline,

disrupting the progress of our children's physical, mental, and emotional
development with the oppressor's tools.

Dr. Joy Degruy calls it "Post Traumatic Slave Syndrome" because the impact of
years of oppression doesn't just go away with integrated lunch counters, schools,
and prisons.

Integration and assimilation have created false freedoms.

But Strong Black Woman, you can break the cycle—

> Understand the system that oppresses you.
> Parent consciously and compassionately.
> Heal old wounds.

When you heal, our ancestors heal, and our children move forward,
less wounded.

Dear Strong Black Woman,

Is your strength a benefit or a burden?

Do you celebrate your lineage:
Harriet
        Sojourner,
                Fannie,
                        Rosa,
                                Michelle.
Do you bask in the glow of your ancestors' resilience?

Or do you hide behind the mask of strength, seething with resentment,
swallowing back tears,

because no one offers
help when you're strong.

Dear Strong Black Woman,

It sometimes feels easier, and safer, to hide our feelings.
Stuff them down, eat over them, work them away,
and keep pushing forward.

But eventually, they catch up to you.
irritability,
anger,
mood swings,
sadness,
hopelessness,

                                        disease.

Strong Black Woman,
feelings are okay.

Strong Black Woman,
it's okay to cry,

Your anger is valid.

Your feelings matter.

Give yourself permission to feel—

Sensations: tingling, pressure, heat, cold
Heart: beating, racing... slowing down.
Breath: moving, stagnant, ebb and flow.
Thoughts: racing, fleeting, absent.

Safely... and... slowly.

Moving them out of your body,
through arms, legs, feet, and fingers,
until you can *finally* breathe,

a little easier.

Dear Strong Black Woman,

Just because you can carry it all,
doesn't mean you have to carry it

alone.

Dear Strong Black Woman,

Our culture says:

>"Black people don't get depressed. We're strong."
>"Pray it away."
>"Don't put your business out in the street."

The truth, Strong Black Woman—we do get depressed, even if we don't give it a name.
Years of struggle and strength eventually takes its toll in the form of fatigue,

the kind of fatigue that you can feel deep down in your bones,
pressing into your shoulders,
weighing on your chest.

Depression:

It is not a character flaw,
not a mood that you can "snap out of,"
not something that can be prayed away.

Depression is not a sign of weakness.

It is:
a mood disorder that affects the brain and the body,
as real as diabetes and heart disease.

It is a condition that can be treated, when we call it by its name.

Dear Strong Black Woman,

The world views you through the lens of white supremacy—

Skin too dark.
Nose too flat.
Hips too wide.
Hair too coarse.
Lips too big...

Through the lens of white supremacy, you are flawed.

But those "flaws" are the sparkles that make up your magic.

So, Strong Black Woman—

Put down the lightening cream,
throw out the waist trainer,
stop the diet.

Accept and embrace these parts of yourself despite societal opinions...

Disrupt the system.

Take money out of white men's pockets.
Put it back into your own.

Capitalism thrives on you believing that you are inherently flawed.

White men get rich off your purchase of the latest *if-you're-white-you're-alright*
hair products and creams.

Put them down, Strong Black Woman,
hold your head high.

Let the revolution begin.

In my eyes, you are
beautiful.

But Strong Black Woman, how do you see yourself?

Dear Strong Black Woman,

There will be times when you look around
and notice that you are the only one in the room.

Brown Skin.
Shea Butter.
Curls poppin'.

When this happens,
remember:

You are worthy.
You are capable.
You matter.

So use your voice.
Take up space.

And next time...
bring a friend.

We rise together.

Dear Strong Black Woman,

Invite laughter.
Savor joy.

No matter how small the moment.

Your resilience depends on it.

Dear Strong Black Woman,

When they said you were "pretty for a black girl,"

they lied.

They wanted to try your pretty on for size and sell it back to you in a lighter shade and a smaller size.

But no one can deny...

The beauty of your full lips.
The confidence in your stride,
powered by full hips and thighs.

From a big, bold 'fro to locks and cornrows,

your hair is magic—
it even stays in place when combed,
holding secrets of resilience from your ancestors
in its kinks and coils.

If you listen closely while you detangle,
you might just hear the whispers of Michelle saying:
Remember, you have within you the strength, patience, and the passion to reach for the stars to change the world.

You might also hear Harriet say:
You're pretty, period.
Don't let them diminish your shine

(...or touch your hair).

Dear Strong Black Woman,

Are you a master chameleon... shapeshifter?

Fracturing yourself to fit into a world that easily accepts whiteness, and condemns blackness—

do you alter the way that you speak... trade African-American Vernacular English for perfectly enunciated words?

Articulate.

Do you straighten your hair... tame it because anything less is "unprofessional?"

Nappy.

Do you carefully monitor your tone of voice to avoid sounding mean, stern, too direct, or serious?

Angry black woman.

Do you shift, and mold, and shape yourself to fit into the box labeled "you're not like those black people?"

Racism.

...and in the process, become frustrated, angry,
            exhausted, depressed.

Strong Black Woman, the greatest fight against white supremacy starts with being true to yourself, in spaces that allow it.

When you can—

            use your voice.
                        Your real one.
            Let your kinky, curly hair be wild and free.
                        Untamed.

Be you when it feels safe, and as often as possible.

Dear Strong Black Woman,

The anger you feel is a legitimate response to:

>Assault.
>Oppression.
>Exploitation.
>And violation, repeated over and over again.

Instead of hiding it, suppressing it, or being ashamed of it:

>Acknowledge it.

>Feel it.

>Find ways to express it.

>Transform it into constructive action.

Your feelings are valid.
>Let no one tell you otherwise.

Dear Strong Black Woman,

Our survival is dependent upon us being more human,
less superhuman.

The superwoman narrative is one left over from chattel slavery—

The explanation white folks used (and continue to use) to justify enslaving our
ancestors and violating our minds, bodies, and spirits.

It is a narrative that we accepted as our own as we took on the matriarchal role in
our
households and communities.

We saw our own strength—independent, hard-working, take mess from no one.

But our strengths can (and maybe have) become our greatest burdens, and this
narrative of the superhuman black woman who feels no pain, does twice as much…
is killing us.

It's time to break the cycle.

Dear Strong Black Woman,

How many times have you gone high when they went low?

How many times did you bite your tongue?
Put up a wall?
Pack your emotions in a box?

How many times did you change your voice,
alter your words, your hair, your clothes,

...yourself, to please your oppressor?

To prove that you are capable, intelligent, and hard-working?

Did you do these things and go on about your business, convinced that they didn't
or wouldn't affect you, then find yourself later feeling depressed, anxious, alone...
exhausted?

Did you do these things because there just wasn't enough time, energy, or safe
space to feel?

Strong Black Woman, it's time for change.

Nothing happens in the body independently.
Your emotions are not separate from your physical body.

Each one of your experiences is met with action by your brain and body.

Repress that action and your emotions, over and over again, and your brain and
body have no choice but to create an action that you can't inhibit,

...illness and dis-ease.

Find your outlet, Strong Black Woman,
it is essential for your resilience.

Dear Strong Black Woman,

Historically speaking, our bodies have not been our own—

Brutalized on slave ships and plantations,
stripped of our bodily autonomy.

And now, as we navigate this modern world,
our colonized bodies are often assumed to be meant for the consumption of others.

Forcing many of us to separate ourselves from our bodies,
numb ourselves from feeling to find relief from the pain of being a black woman
in a society where we are at the bottom of the hierarchical ladder.

When it's safe to awaken, Strong Black Woman,

Feel the life inside your body,

reclaim the parts of yourself that were taken from you.

Feel your heart beating, each pulse and vibration.

(Vitality)

Whispering...

this is my body.

this is my body.

this is my body.

It belongs to me.

Dear Strong Black Woman,

We've been taught to carry the burdens of everyone,
bandage the wounds of others
while bleeding from our own.

If you are going to survive
thrive,

you must tend to your own wounds.
Heal.

The strength you garner from your own healing
can be used to heal your community.

Dear Strong Black Woman,

How is your heart?

Really, how is it?

Is it weighed down with anger, resentment, and sadness,
or are you able to make room for love, forgiveness, gratitude, and joy?

I ask because heart disease kills nearly 50,000 of us each year.

Stress.
Inflammation.
A heart and arteries that demand to be fed.

More blood.

Activating blood cell fragments,
platelets.

Likely to clump and form clots in the bloodstream.

Protect your heart, Strong Black Woman.
Nourish it.
And treat yourself well.

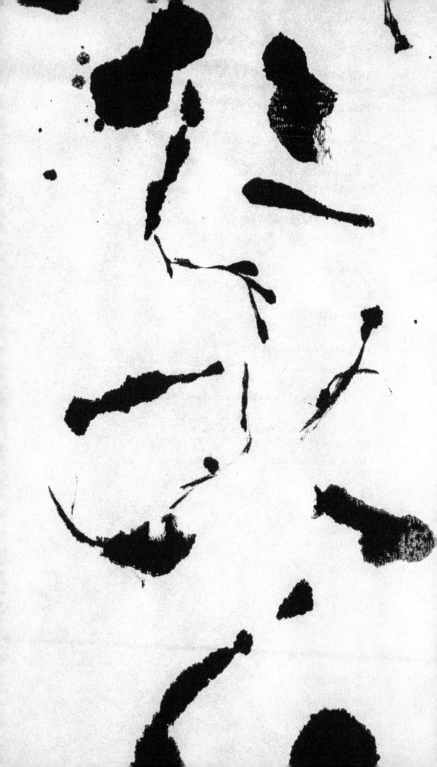

Dear Strong Black Woman,

Remember to breathe.

Feel the pleasure of your inhale as it tickles the inside of your nose.

Notice the warmth of your exhale as it lingers on your tongue

...l o n g and easy.

Taste the freedom your ancestors wanted for you

...sweet like honey.

Dear Strong Black Woman,

Your body is the most honest part of your being.
It doesn't lie.
It can't.

Its needs are so primal and basic—food, water, sleep, rest, love.

Care.

When you deprive it of these things, it will let you know—stomach pains, headaches, unbearable fatigue.

A deep longing that can only be filled with hugs, touch, a listening ear.

Your body even communicates its fears.

The things you may never say aloud, your body says—shallow breaths, racing heart, insomnia

...depression and anxiety.

We can tell one story with our mouths,

"I'm fine."

"I can handle it."

But the body... your wise and beautiful body,
isn't capable of fakin' the funk, no matter how much you want it to.

What truth is your body speaking right now?

Dear Strong Black Woman,

Building a wall around your heart,
so thick and so hard that love can't enter....

That helps for a time.

But only briefly...

until love stops trying to build a door,
and leaves you.

Alone.

Dear Strong Black Woman,

Always remember:

The need and desire to heal does not mean you are broken.
It means you are human.

Perfectly imperfect,
and whole.

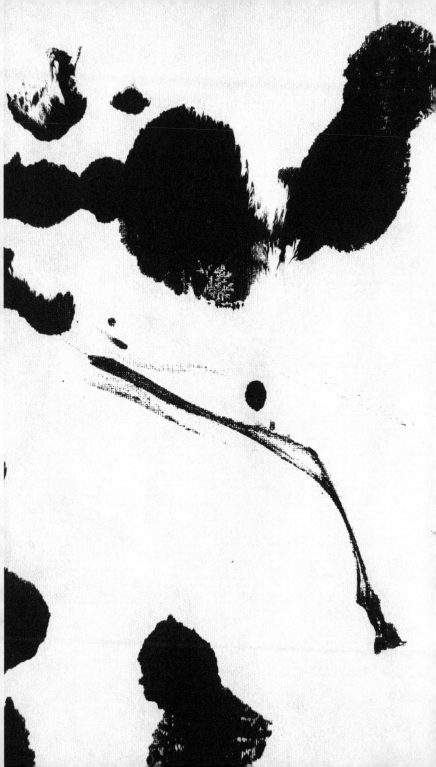

Dear Strong Black Woman,

Reach out for help
before the trauma of being a woman in a black body
becomes too heavy a burden to bear.

It often feels better to be supported,
than alone.

Dear Strong Black Woman,

You don't have to speak to heal.

Move.
Create.
Sing.
Play.

In the absence of therapy our ancestors:

"Wade in the water,"
danced the Juba,
were moved by the Holy Ghost.

They found moments of lightness and hope,
and savored them.

Because freedom isn't just physical
and sometimes words aren't enough
to process and express the pain.

Dear Strong Black Woman,

We've been called everything, but our names.
Assumed to be less than human, one dimensional.

We've been compared to Jezebel,
described as lascivious creatures,
governed by erotic desires.

We've been assumed angry for expressing our thoughts, beliefs, and feelings,
with anything other than a smile on our face
and softness in our voices.

We've been called mammies,
"Happy and content servants."

Called everything... but our names.

Your name, Strong Black Woman,
whether Karen or Shaqueshia, Jennifer or Shalameisha...

Say it loud.
Say it proud.

Claim yourself as an individual, multidimensional, and complex.

In a system that thrives on our collective otherness,
saying your name is resistance.

It is power.

Dear Strong Black Woman,

Someone else has been writing our story.

In their story, we are:
workhorses
mammies
welfare queens
hot mamas

...angry for no reason and *built* for struggle.

In their story, we are invulnerable and feel no pain.

Born slaves.

They need this to justify slavery,
institutionalized racism,
oppression.

We need to know this narrative because knowing "where we came from" affords us with the awareness that we need to begin to separate the truth from the lies.

The Strong Black Woman is not a lie—many of us routinely do and cope with more than could or should be expected, because we have to.

The lie is that we were *built* for this.
That built into our DNA is the ability to endure constant stress and strain.

The truth:

Each time we tend, befriend, mend, and keep our stress and emotions in, we pay with our physical and mental health.

Strong Black Woman,

REST.

In a world that tells us our value is based on how much we produce, rest is our resistance.

It is also the foundation of good health and healing.

Dear Strong Black Woman,

What are you hungry for—
        what would fill you up,
        nourish you,
        soothe the cravings deep down in your soul?

Pause.

And ask, in service of your brain, your body, and your spirit.
Because you deserve pleasure.

You deserve joy.

You deserve the deepest of nourishment.

Awareness, acknowledgement, and asking are the way receive it.

Dear Strong Black Woman,

You are strong.
You are resilient.
You are beautiful.
You are magic.

You are also 100% human.

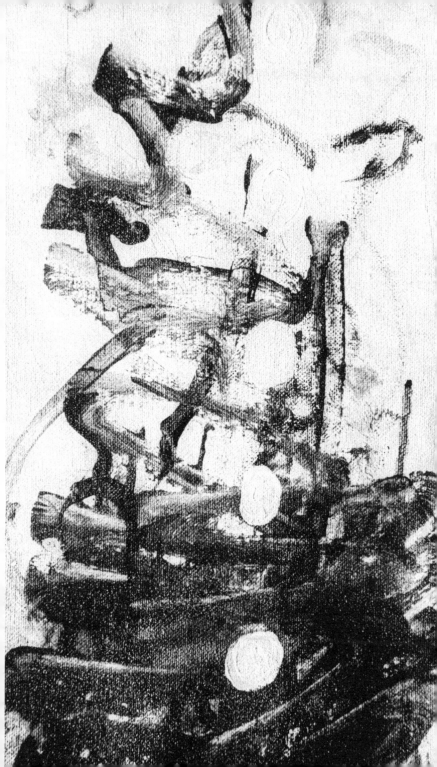

Dear Strong Black Woman,

It's okay to love yourself,
first.

Dear Strong Black Woman,

Pause for a moment and listen

to the sounds of your ancestors.

Chanting:

"Aye..."

"Aye..."

"Aye..."

They are cheering you on.
Because even on your worst days,

you are the manifestation of their wildest dreams.

about the author

Jennifer Sterling is a black woman. She is also a Registered Dance/Movement Psychotherapist and the creator of The Bodyful Healing Project, an initiative that offers support and resources to black women living with depression. Having witnessed the adverse effects of oppressive systems on black women in her community and through her own lived experience, Jennifer has made it her mission to help reduce the stigma around mental illness within black communities, as well as educate others on the effects of oppression on black women's bodies.